·TESCO· COOKERY· COLLECTION·
MEALS IN MINUTES

TESCO

Published exclusively for Tesco Stores Ltd,
Delamare Road, Cheshunt, Herts. EN8 9SL
by Cathay Books, 59 Grosvenor Street, London W1

First published 1985

© Cathay Books 1985

ISBN 0 86178 309 3

Printed in Hong Kong

ACKNOWLEDGEMENTS

The publishers would like to thank the following companies
for their kindness in providing materials and equipment
used in the photography for this book.
David Mellor, 26 James Street, London WC2 and 4 Sloane Square, London SW1;
Elizabeth David, 46 Bourne Street, London SW1;
General Trading Co, 144 Sloane St, London SW1;
Harrods and Way In, Knightsbridge, London SW1;
Reject Shop, King's Road SW3
Mappin & Webb, Regent Street, London W1;
The Design Council, Haymarket, London W1

We would also like to thank the following who
were concerned in the preparation of the book.

Series Art Director Pedro Prá-Lopez
Editor Beverley Le Blanc
Photographer Alan Duns; James Jackson (pages 7, 25, 37, 53, 57)
Stylist Paula Lovell
Food prepared for photography by Emma Codrington; Joyce Harrison;
Dolly Meers

CONTENTS

NOTE

Standard spoon measurements are used in all recipes

1 tablespoon (tbls) = one 15 ml spoon
1 teaspoon (tsp) = one 5 ml spoon
All spoon measures are level

All eggs are sizes 3 or 4 (standard) unless otherwise stated.

For all recipes, quantities are given in both
metric and imperial measures. Follow either set
but not a mixture of both, as they are not interchangeable.

We set up our Consumer Advisory Service in response to the many pleas for information and cooking ideas we received from our customers. It is run by our team of qualified home economists who answer queries, offer practical advice on cookery and the home and give talks and demonstrations on new products and equipment.
The resounding success of the service and the continued demand for more and more recipes and information has now prompted us to produce our own special range of Tesco Cookery Books.
Our series starts with 12 books, each one focusing on an area that our customers have shown particular interest in. Each book contains practical background information on the chosen subject and concentrates on a wide selection of carefully tested recipes, each one illustrated in colour.

Meals in Minutes contains an interesting variety of recipes from impressive dinner party dishes to quick snacks and no-cook meals. They can all be prepared in under an hour and many take 20 minutes or less. We offer advice on planning, and time-saving tips together with serving ideas and variations for many recipes. If your cooking has to fit into a busy schedule this special Tesco collection will give you more time to yourself, while enabling you to produce attractive and nutritious meals whatever the occasion. I very much hope you will enjoy looking through the pages which follow, trying out the recipes and above all tasting and enjoying the results. Happy Cooking!

Carey Dennis, senior home economist, Tesco Stores Ltd.

INTRODUCTION

Meals in Minutes has been compiled specifically for people who have to cook in a hurry but who still want to prepare delicious and attractive food. The Suppers and Snacks chapter contains recipes that can be prepared in no more than 20 minutes and are suitable for all occasions from starters to vegetable accompaniments for a dinner party or a one-dish supper at the end of a hectic day. The Main Meals chapter contains more substantial dishes but they still take no more than 40 minutes to prepare, and the tempting recipes in the Desserts chapter also take only 40 minutes or less to make. There is even a section of no-cook recipes!

Stocking a store cupboard

With a little careful thought you can use your store cupboard to save time not only when you are in a real hurry but also when making everyday meals. For example, cans of peeled tomatoes save a great deal of time when preparing stews, casseroles, soups and sauces; cans of condensed soups can be made into sauces for chicken, fish and rice dishes, and condensed consommés are handy to use as meat glazes and can even be chilled and chopped to be mixed with cold meats and salad.

Foods that are handy to have include:
- canned fish, such as tuna, and mackerel fillets packed in oil or brine
- canned vegetables, such as tomatoes, sweetcorn, pimientos, asparagus tips and a wide variety of beans
- condensed soups and consommés
- soup and sauce mixes
- dried milk and UHT or canned cream
- pasta and pulses
- canned and bottled fruits

Using your freezer

A well-stocked freezer can also help save time. Frozen vegetables can be cooked straight from the freezer. Sorbets and ice creams need only soften after being taken from the freezer, and fast-thawing fruits like raspberries or blackcurrants make quick desserts or toppings.

You can save yourself a great deal of baking time by stocking your freezer with frozen pastry and pastry cases. Frozen bread dough loaves can be cooked without defrosting first. And, when you make home-made bread, double the quantity of dough and put the extra in the freezer for spur-of-the-moment baking.

Try these quick tips to help you use your freezer to its best advantage:
- Grate hard cheese, freeze in portions and use straight from the freezer for sauces and grilled toppings.
- Freeze finely chopped herbs in season in ice cube trays with a little water to provide a fresh herb garnish for soups or sauces in the winter.
- Wine left over from a meal can be frozen in ice cube trays and used when making casseroles and for marinades or sauces.

Careful planning

Being able to cope with unexpected situations like leaving the office late and last minute guests is one thing but careful advance planning of daily meals should also mean you do not have to spend too much valuable time in the kitchen. Tackle as much as you can beforehand. With just a little bit of planning you can save time on your shopping trips and in the kitchen so that cooking remains a pleasure rather than a chore.

NO COOK MEALS

Gazpacho

SERVES 4

50 g (2 oz) fresh white breadcrumbs
3 tbls red wine vinegar
2 large tomatoes, roughly chopped
½ cucumber, chopped
1 green pepper, cored, seeded and
  chopped
2 Spanish onions, chopped
1 clove garlic, crushed
4 tbls olive oil
350 ml (12 fl oz) tomato juice, chilled
300 ml (½ pint) cold water
salt and pepper
4 ice cubes
To serve
1 onion, finely chopped
¼ cucumber, finely chopped
1 small tomato, chopped
½ red and ½ green pepper, seeded
  and chopped
50 g (2 oz) croûtons

Soak the breadcrumbs in the vinegar in a small bowl.

Mix together the tomatoes, cucumber, green pepper, onion and garlic and purée in a blender or food processor. Pour into a bowl.

Add the breadcrumbs to the purée and gradually stir in the oil, drop by drop. Stir in the tomato juice and water and season to taste.

Chill in the refrigerator for at least 3 hours.

Adjust the seasoning to taste and pour into chilled individual soup bowls with an ice cube in each. Hand round the chopped vegetables and croûtons separately.

Serving ideas: This traditional Spanish soup is filling and almost a meal in itself. Serve with hot crusty French bread or herb bread and olives.

Jugged kippers

SERVES 4

4 kippers
approx 1.2 litres (2 pints) boiling water
50 g (2 oz) butter
pepper

Place the kippers in a deep heatproof bowl and cover all but the tails with the water.

Leave for 3-5 minutes, then drain the kippers and transfer to a heated serving dish.

Dot the kippers with the butter, season with freshly ground black pepper and serve immediately.

Serving idea: These kippers are ideal for a special breakfast or brunch. Serve with scrambled eggs garnished with parsley, grilled tomatoes and mushrooms and toasted wholemeal bread.

Cucumber tarragon soup

SERVES 4

1½ large cucumbers, peeled and
  chopped
450 g (15.9 oz) carton natural low-fat
  yoghurt
1 tbls chopped fresh tarragon or 1 tsp
  dried tarragon
salt and pepper
8 cucumber slices, to garnish
4 sprigs fresh tarragon

Place all the ingredients in a blender and process until smooth and frothy.

Pour into chilled individual soup bowls, garnish each with 2 cucumber slices and a sprig of fresh tarragon.

● Top: Gazpacho; Centre: Cucumber tarragon soup; Bottom: Jugged kippers

Melon and prawn salad

SERVES 4

1 honeydew melon, halved and
   seeded
450 g (1 lb) peeled prawns, thawed if
   frozen
Fresh mint sprigs, to garnish
For the dressing
1 tbls vegetable oil
1 tbls white wine vinegar
1 tsp caster sugar
2 tbls single cream
salt and pepper

Scoop out the melon flesh with a melon baller or teaspoon, working over a large bowl to catch all the juices.

Place the melon balls in the bowl with the juice. Rinse the prawns under cold running water and pat dry with absorbent paper. Add to the melon balls, cover with cling film and chill in the refrigerator while making the dressing.

Place all the dressing ingredients in a screw-top jar and shake vigorously until thoroughly blended. Chill until ready to serve.

To serve, place the Melon and prawn salad in individual salad bowls. Place a mint sprig on top of each salad to garnish. Shake the dressing again, pour into a jug and hand round separately.

Serving idea: This salad is an impressive starter for an elegant dinner party. Because it is so light it is suitable to precede a rich main course.

• Melon and prawn salad

Carrot and fruit salad

SERVES 4

4 carrots, grated
1 dessert apple, peeled and chopped
2 tbls lemon juice
1 small orange, peeled and
   segmented
25 g (1 oz) full fat soft cheese
1 tbls single cream
1 tbls chopped fresh parsley
salt and white pepper
pinch of paprika

Combine the carrots and apple and sprinkle with half the lemon juice.

Remove all the white pith from the orange segments and add to the bowl. Cover with cling film and chill for 30 minutes or longer.

Beat together the full fat soft cheese, cream and remaining lemon juice and stir in the parsley, salt and white pepper to taste and the paprika.

Place the salad in 4 individual bowls. Spoon a little dressing over each and serve immediately.

Serving ideas: This salad helps make the most of cold leftover chicken or ham. For a buffet selection serve it with the Danish cold table (p.13), the Melon and prawn salad (p.8), and the Tuna bean bowl (p.11).

Variation: For a more exotic flavour use lime juice instead of lemon juice and sprinkle over 25 g (1 oz) of coarse desiccated coconut.

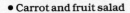

● Carrot and fruit salad

• Left: Cold curried chicken; Right: Tuna bean bowl

Cold curried chicken

SERVES 4

225 g (8 oz) thick mayonnaise
2 tsp curry paste
2 tsp apricot jam
2 tsp lemon juice
salt and pepper
4 crisp lettuce leaves
4 cooked chicken breasts, boned and
    skinned
1 tbls chopped fresh coriander or
    coriander sprigs, to garnish

In a bowl, thoroughly combine the mayonnaise, curry paste, apricot jam, lemon juice and salt and freshly ground black pepper to taste.

Rinse the lettuce leaves under cold running water and pat dry with absorbent paper.

Line a serving dish with the lettuce leaves and arrange the chicken breasts on top. Spoon a portion of the curry mayonnaise over each chicken breast and sprinkle with the chopped coriander or garnish with coriander sprigs. Serve the remaining mayonnaise separately in a small bowl.

Serving idea: Accompany the chicken with a tossed green salad, sliced banana mixed with desiccated coconut and warm pitta bread.
Variation: This dish may also be made with other poultry such as leftover cold roast turkey or duck.

10

Tuna bean bowl

SERVES 4

198 g (7 oz) can red kidney beans,
  drained
220 g (7¾ oz) can butter beans,
  drained
198 g (7 oz) can chick peas, drained
¼ tsp dried marjoram
¼ tsp dried thyme
4 tbls chopped fresh parsley
198 g (7 oz) can tuna, drained and
  flaked
For the dressing
4 tbls lemon juice
6 tbls olive oil
1 onion, finely chopped
1 garlic clove, crushed
4 tsp Dijon mustard
salt and freshly ground
  black pepper

Rinse the pulses under cold running
water, drain again and place in a large
salad bowl. Sprinkle with the dried
marjoram and thyme.

Place half the parsley and all the
dressing ingredients, with plenty of
seasoning, in a screw-top jar and shake
vigorously until thoroughly blended.

Pour the dressing over the pulses
and toss gently to coat evenly. Cover
with cling film and chill in the refrigerator until ready to serve.

To serve, add the tuna and stir gently
to mix. Sprinkle with the remaining
chopped parsley.

Serving ideas: This salad makes a
complete light meal if served with
crusty bread and a selection of
cheeses. Alternatively, serve as a dinner
party starter with hot garlic or herb
bread.

Speedy liver pâté

SERVES 4

450 g (1 lb) soft liver sausage
75 g (3 oz) butter, softened
1 tbls finely chopped chives
1 tbls brandy
1 tsp dried sage
salt and pepper

In a bowl, beat together the liver sausage and butter until thoroughly blended and smooth.

Beat in the chives, brandy and sage and season to taste.

Place the pâté in a small bowl or pâté mould and smooth the top, or fork a pattern across the surface.

Serve immediately or cover with cling film and chill in the refrigerator until ready to serve.

Serving idea: If friends drop in unexpectedly for drinks, use this pâté to make canapés – spread on savoury biscuits or toast triangles and top with dill pickle or tomato. For a special occasion leave in the mould or dish and cover with a layer of aspic jelly.

Iced prawn soup

SERVES 4

397 g (14 oz) can cream of celery soup
450 ml (¾ pint) tomato juice
pinch of cayenne pepper
2 tbls lemon juice
100 g (4 oz) prawns, thawed if frozen,
*   peeled and chopped*
salt and pepper
To garnish
4 tbls single cream
2 tbls chopped fresh parsley

Thoroughly combine the soup, tomato juice, cayenne pepper and lemon juice in a bowl. Stir in the prawns and season to taste.

Cover with cling film and chill in the refrigerator for at least 30 minutes before serving.

To serve, pour the soup into individual chilled serving bowls, swirl 1 tbls of cream over each and sprinkle with the chopped parsley.

Serving idea: Serve with Melba toast as a starter to a summer dinner.

Danish cold table

SERVES 4

1 large dessert apple, unpeeled and
   thinly sliced
1 tbls lemon juice
8 slices dark or light rye or
   pumpernickel bread
100g (4 oz) unsalted butter, softened
225g (8 oz) thick mayonnaise
100g (4 oz) Danish blue cheese,
   crumbled
4 soused herrings, drained
100g (4 oz) sliced cooked ham
100g (4 oz) peeled prawns, rinsed
4 hard-boiled eggs, sliced
8-12 cucumber slices
8-12 tomato slices
fresh dill sprigs
parsley sprigs

Brush the apple slices with lemon juice to prevent discoloration.

Arrange the bread and the toppings in dishes on the table so that guests can help themselves to make open sandwiches with the combination of toppings they prefer.

Serving ideas: In Denmark open sandwiches are served with chilled lager or schnapps, a strong drink made from potatoes and grain.

Variations: All the salad garnishes and toppings may be varied. Other Danish smørrebrød toppings may include thinly sliced smoked salmon, onion rings, Danish caviar or smoked fish roe, and crumbled grilled bacon. Vary the amount of each ingredient depending on the number of people to serve.

● Iced prawn soup; Speedy liver pâté; Danish cold table

Stuffed avocado pâté

SERVES 4

2 avocados, halved and stoned
4 hard-boiled eggs, chopped
2 tbls white wine vinegar
1 garlic clove, crushed
1 tsp chopped fresh parsley
1 tsp lemon juice
salt and pepper
4 crisp lettuce leaves, to serve
4 parsley sprigs, to garnish

Taking care not to pierce the skins, remove the avocado flesh and place in a bowl. Reserve the skins.

Mash the avocado flesh with the eggs, vinegar, garlic, parsley, lemon juice, salt and plenty of freshly ground black pepper in a food processor or blender, until smooth.

Carefully spoon the avocado mixture into the skins. Place on individual plates lined with lettuce leaves and garnish each avocado half with a parsley sprig. Serve at once.

·*Serving ideas:* This pâté can also be served in ramekins. Accompany with fingers of buttered toast or, if you prefer, with crisp-bread or melba toast.

Pipérade

SERVES 4

4 tbls tomato juice
1 red pepper, cored, seeded and sliced
1 green pepper, cored, seeded and
    sliced
1 large onion, sliced
2 garlic cloves, crushed
4 tomatoes, skinned, seeded and
    chopped
½ tsp dried thyme
½ tsp dried oregano
salt and pepper
4 large eggs, beaten

Place the tomato juice, peppers, onion
and garlic in a non-stick saucepan and
cook gently for 5 minutes, stirring occasionally, until softened.

Add the tomatoes, herbs and salt and
pepper to taste and cook for a further 5

minutes, stirring frequently.

Pour in the eggs and cook gently for
about 5 minutes, stirring constantly,
until the eggs are cooked.

Transfer to a heated serving dish and
serve at once.

Spinach soup with croûtons

SERVES 4

25 g (1 oz) margarine or butter
1 small onion, finely chopped
1 tbls cornflour
450 ml (¾ pint) chicken stock
salt and pepper
pinch of nutmeg
225 g (8 oz) frozen chopped spinach
vegetable oil, for frying
2 slices day-old bread, crusts removed
    and cubed
120 ml (4 fl oz) milk
2 tbls double cream

Melt the margarine in a large saucepan, add the onion and cook gently for 5
minutes until softened. Add the cornflour and cook for 1 further minute,
stirring constantly.

Gradually stir in the stock, salt and
pepper and nutmeg and bring to the
boil. Add the frozen spinach, cover and
simmer for about 10 minutes, stirring
occasionally.

Meanwhile, make the croûtons. Heat
a depth of 5 mm (¼ inch) of oil in a
frying pan, add the bread cubes and fry
over moderately high heat, turning,
until golden brown. Drain on absorbent paper and set aside.

Purée the spinach soup in a blender,
then return to the pan. Adjust the seasoning to taste, stir in the milk and
return gently to boiling point.

Pour the soup into heated individual
soup bowls, swirl a portion of cream
over each and hand the croûtons
separately in a bowl.

● Left: Spinach soup with croûtons;
Centre: Pipérade; Right: Stuffed avocado
pâté

15

Omelettes à la crème

SERVES 4

225 g (8 oz) Cheddar cheese, grated
6 tbls single cream
12 eggs
275 ml (9 fl oz) water
salt and pepper
100 g (4 oz) butter
8 canned asparagus spears

These ingredients are enough to make 4 single omelettes or 2 omelettes large enough to serve 2 persons each. The following instructions are for two large omelettes.

Heat the grill to high.

Mix together half the cheese and half the cream.

In a separate bowl, beat 6 eggs with half the water and season to taste.

Melt half the butter in a large omelette pan and when sizzling pour in the egg mixture. When the omelette begins to set, draw the edges gently into the centre of the pan and allow the liquid egg to run underneath, using a wooden spatula. When the omelette is almost set, but still creamy, spread it out to the sides of the pan and allow to set completely.

Spoon half the cheese and cream mixture down the centre of the omelette. Arrange 4 asparagus spears on one half of the omelette and fold the other half over, to cover. Slide the omelette on to a flameproof plate.

Cover the omelette with the remaining cheese mixture. Place under the grill for several seconds until the cheese is bubbling.

Keep warm while preparing the second omelette in the same way.

Serving ideas: Serve with toasted wholewheat bread or as a main meal with tomatoes and baked potatoes.

• Omelettes à la crème; Mexican rarebit

Mexican rarebit

SERVES 4

25 g (1 oz) margarine or unsalted
   butter
1 onion, finely chopped
1 garlic clove, crushed
1 green pepper, cored, seeded and
   chopped
397 g (14 oz) can red kidney beans,
   drained
439 g (15½ oz) can baked beans in
   tomato sauce
4 tbls tomato ketchup
1 tbls Worcestershire sauce
salt and pepper
2 tsp mild chilli powder
175 g (6 oz) Cheddar or other hard
   cheese, grated
4 slices hot toast, buttered

Melt the margarine in a large frying
pan. Add the onion, garlic and green
pepper and fry gently for 5 minutes
until softened.

Rinse the kidney beans under cold
running water, drain again and add to
the frying pan with the baked beans in
their sauce, the ketchup, Worcestershire sauce, salt and pepper to taste
and the chilli powder. Cook for a further 5 minutes, stirring occasionally.

Stir in the cheese and cook for a
further 3 minutes, stirring constantly
until the cheese is melted.

Place the toast on 4 heated individual
plates and spoon the bean and cheese
mixture on top. Serve immediately.

Serving ideas: Serve with a refreshing
tomato salad or with a crisp green lettuce and sweet red pepper salad.

Cheese fondue

SERVES 4

1 French loaf
2 garlic cloves, halved
350 g (12 oz) Gruyère cheese, grated
150 ml (¼ pint) milk
450 ml (¾ pint) dry white wine
1 tbls Kirsch
salt and pepper.

Heat the oven to 180°C, 350°F, Gas Mark 4.

Place the French loaf in the oven to warm through while preparing the fondue.

Rub the sides and base of a fondue pot with the cut sides of the garlic cloves. Add the cheese and milk and cook over a low heat until the cheese melts and the mixture is smooth.

Gradually stir in the wine and Kirsch and season. Continue to heat the fondue without allowing it to come to the boil, making sure it does not stick to the base of the pot.

Meanwhile, remove the French loaf from the oven and cut into 2.5 cm (1 inch) cubes.

Place the fondue pot over a lighted spirit burner and the bread cubes in a serving bowl. Serve with long fondue forks to spear the bread cubes and then dip into the cheese mixture.

Serving idea: The Swiss often follow a fondue with a fruit-based dessert. Complete this meal with Pineapple boats (see page 54) or a fresh fruit salad.

● Left: Cheese fondue; Centre: Pork and prawns, Japanese style; Right: Prawns Newburg

Prawns Newburg

SERVES 4

2.25 litres (4 pints) water
4 tsp salt
100 g (4 oz) long-grain rice
50 g (2 oz) butter
350 g (12 oz) peeled prawns
6 tbls Madeira or sweet sherry
pinch of paprika
salt and pepper
2 egg yolks
142 ml (5 fl oz) carton single cream
2 tbls chopped fresh parsley
a little paprika, to finish
parsley sprigs, to garnish

Bring the water to the boil with the salt in a saucepan, add the rice and boil for 12-15 minutes until just tender.

Meanwhile, melt the butter in a large saucepan, add the prawns and fry gently for 3-4 minutes. Stir in the Madeira and cook for a further 3 minutes until reduced. Add the paprika and season.

Beat the egg yolks with the cream and gradually whisk into the pan. Heat through very gently until thickened, but on no account allow to boil.

Drain the cooked rice and rinse with boiling water, then drain again. Stir the parsley into the rice and place on heated individual plates. Spoon over the prawn mixture, dust with a little paprika, garnish with parsley sprigs and serve immediately.

Pork and prawns, Japanese style

SERVES 4

225 g (8 oz) vermicelli
1 tbls vegetable oil
1 garlic clove, crushed
1 small onion, sliced
225 g (8 oz) pork tenderloin, thinly
    sliced
100 g (4 oz) peeled prawns
salt and pepper
1 tbls chopped spring onion, to garnish
For the sauce
2 tbls light soy sauce
2 tbls tomato ketchup
1 tsp finely grated lemon rind
2 tbls lemon juice

Cook the vermicelli in boiling, salted water according to packet instructions, until just tender. Then drain.

Meanwhile, heat the oil in a wok or large frying pan. Add the garlic and onion and stir-fry for about 2 minutes.

Add the pork, prawns and seasoning. Stir-fry for a further 4 minutes until the pork is almost cooked through.

Combine all the sauce ingredients and add to the wok with the noodles. Stir-fry for a further 2 minutes until the pork is cooked through and all the ingredients are hot.

Transfer to a heated dish, garnish with the chopped spring onions and serve immediately.

19

• Left: Broad beans with garlic sausage; Right: Smoked haddock bake

Smoked haddock bake

SERVES 4

750 g (1 1/2 lb) smoked haddock fillet
300 ml (1/2 pint) milk
1 tsp grated lemon rind
salt and pepper
2 tsp cornflour
1 tsp water
25 g (1 oz) margarine or butter
lemon slices and parsley sprigs, to
    garnish

Cut the smoked haddock fillet into 4 equal portions and place in a saucepan with the milk, lemon rind and salt and pepper. Cover and simmer very gently for 8-10 minutes, until the fish is cooked through.

Blend the cornflour to a smooth paste with the water.

Using a fish slice, carefully remove the fish from the pan, transfer to heated serving dish and keep warm.

Stir the cornflour paste into the milk in the pan and bring to the boil, stirring constantly, until the sauce has thickened. Add the margarine or butter and stir until melted.

Spoon the sauce over the fish, garnish with the lemon slices and parsley and serve at once.

Serving idea: Arrange toast triangles around the edge of the dish, if liked.

Broad beans with garlic sausage

SERVES 4

450 g (1 lb) frozen broad beans
25 (1 oz) margarine or butter
2 shallots or 1 onion, chopped
100 g (4 oz) garlic sausage, chopped
2 tsp chopped fresh savory
salt and pepper
142 ml (5 fl oz) carton single cream
1 tbls chopped fresh parsley, to
    garnish

Cook the broad beans according to the instructions on the packet, then drain.

Meanwhile, melt the margarine in a saucepan, add the shallots and fry gently for 5 minutes until softened. Add the sausage and fry for a further 2-3 minutes, stirring frequently.

Add the beans to the pan with the savory and salt and pepper. Stir gently to mix, then stir in the cream and heat through gently without allowing the mixture to boil.

Transfer to a heated serving dish, sprinkle the top with parsley and serve immediately.

Serving ideas: Serve as a light lunch or supper dish with crusty bread and butter, or as an accompaniment to grilled pork or lamb chops.

Variations: Shelled fresh broad beans can be used but allow 20-25 minutes for cooking. Use chopped bacon instead of the sausage but fry it first before adding the shallots or onions. If savory is not available use more chopped parsley instead.

Tangy fried chicken livers and broccoli

SERVES 4

2 tbls vegetable oil
2 tbls butter
2 garlic cloves, crushed
225 g (8 oz) mushrooms, thinly sliced
450 g (1 lb) chicken livers, trimmed
    and chopped
100 g (4 oz) broccoli, chopped
1 tbls grated orange rind
4 tbls orange juice
2 tbls dry sherry
pinch of ground ginger
salt and pepper
2 tbls chopped fresh parsley, to
    garnish (optional)

Heat the oil and butter in a large frying pan. Add the garlic and cook gently, stirring, for 1 minute.

Add the mushrooms and chicken livers and cook for 5 minutes, stirring occasionally, until the chicken livers are browned on all sides.

Add the broccoli, orange rind and juice, sherry and ginger. Season with salt and plenty of pepper.

Bring to the boil, reduce the heat, cover and simmer for 5-6 minutes or until the broccoli is just tender.

Adjust the seasoning to taste and transfer to a serving dish. Sprinkle the chicken with the parsley, if liked, and serve immediately.

Serving ideas: Serve on a bed of hot boiled rice with a little butter added or with fine rice noodles.

In a bowl, combine the soy sauce, stock, sherry, vinegar and cornflour, to make a smooth paste.

Heat the oil in a wok or deep frying pan. Add the onion and garlic and fry for 30 seconds. Add the pork and bean sprouts, season to taste and stir-fry for a further minute.

Add the soy sauce mixture, stir-fry for a further 1½ minutes and serve.

Serving idea: Serve on a bed of freshly boiled Chinese egg noodles.
Variations: Thinly sliced beef can be substituted for the pork and 100 g (4 oz) thinly sliced mushrooms can be added to either version with an extra 1 tsp sherry.

Tuna salad, Chinese style

SERVES 4

8 Chinese lettuce leaves, shredded
4 radishes, thinly sliced
1 bunch spring onions, finely chopped
1 medium cucumber, cut into
*   matchstick strips*
50 g (2 oz) fresh bean sprouts
4-8 canned water chestnuts, drained
*   and thinly sliced*
2 × 198 g (7 oz) cans tuna, drained
*   and flaked*
For the dressing
1 tbls light soy sauce
2 tbls vegetable oil
1 tbls fresh orange juice
1 tsp ground ginger
½ tsp caster sugar
salt and pepper

Line 4 individual serving plates with the lettuce leaves.

Arrange the radishes, spring onions, cucumber sticks, beansprouts and water chestnuts over the lettuce, then top with the tuna.

In a jug, combine the dressing ingredients and blend thoroughly together with a fork.

Serve the salads with the dressing handed separately.

• Tuna salad, Chinese style; Tangy fried chicken livers and broccoli; Stir-fried pork with bean sprouts

Stir-fried pork with bean sprouts

SERVES 4

2 tbls light soy sauce
4 tbls chicken stock
2 tsp dry sherry
2 tbls white wine vinegar
2 tsp cornflour
5 tbls vegetable oil
2 tbls finely chopped onion
1 garlic clove, crushed
225 g (8 oz) lean pork fillet, in strips
100 g (4 oz) bean sprouts
salt and pepper

Cauliflower cheese with almonds

SERVES 4

1 large cauliflower, broken into florets
1 litre (1¾ pints) water
1 tsp salt
40 g (1½ oz) packet cheese sauce mix
300 ml (½ pint) milk
40 g (1½ oz) margarine or butter
4 tbls fresh wholemeal breadcrumbs
25 g (1 oz) flaked almonds
1 garlic clove, crushed
salt and pepper
2 tbls chopped fresh parsley, to garnish (optional)

Cook the cauliflower in a large saucepan of boiling salted water for about 10 minutes, until tender, then drain.

Meanwhile, put the cheese sauce mix into a small saucepan, stir in the milk and bring to the boil. Simmer for 1-2 minutes until the sauce has thickened, stirring occasionally, then set aside and keep warm.

Melt the margarine in a frying pan, add the breadcrumbs, almonds and garlic and fry over moderate heat, stirring, until browned. Season with salt and plenty of pepper and remove the pan from the heat.

Place the cauliflower in a heated serving dish, pour over the cheese sauce and top with the fried breadcrumb mixture. Sprinkle with the parsley, if using, and serve immediately.

Serving idea: This dish goes well with Mackerel with gooseberry sauce. (See page 28). It also makes a complete meal in itself especially if served with baked potatoes followed by a crisp, green salad.

Variation: Beat 2 egg yolks into the cheese sauce and add a pinch of cayenne pepper, or instead of a cheese sauce mix, use a curry sauce mix and garnish with fresh chopped coriander.

Leeks niçoise

SERVES 4

4 tbls olive oil
1 kg (2 lb) young leeks, trimmed and cut into 2.5 cm (1 inch) pieces
salt and pepper
227 g (8 oz) tomatoes, skinned and chopped
1 garlic clove, crushed
1 tbls chopped fresh parsley
about 1 tbls lemon juice
flat-leaf parsley, to garnish

Heat the oil in a flameproof casserole, add the leeks and fry over moderate heat, stirring, until lightly coloured. Season, adding plenty of freshly ground black pepper, then cover and cook gently for about 10 minutes or until the leeks are just tender.

Using a slotted spoon, remove the leeks from the casserole and set aside on a plate.

Add the tomatoes, garlic and parsley to the casserole and cook briskly for 3-5 minutes, stirring constantly, until the tomatoes are reduced to a thick pulp. Adjust the seasoning and add lemon juice to taste.

Return the leeks to the casserole, cook gently for 1 further minute. Garnish with a sprig or two of flat-leaf parsley and serve immediately.

Serving ideas: This dish goes well with plainly grilled chicken or fish. It is also good served chilled as a first course with warm garlic or herb bread. It can be made in advance, covered with cling film and chilled in the refrigerator until required.

Variations: Two drained and finely chopped anchovy fillets may be added to the casserole with the tomatoes. Or, stoned black olives (particularly the large kalamatas from Greece) and a little grated orange peel may also be included.

• Leeks niçoise; Cauliflower cheese with almonds

Tagliatelle with mushrooms and cream

SERVES 4

1.75 litres (3½ pints) water
2 tsp salt
1 tbls olive oil
350 g (12 oz) spinach tagliatelle
75 g (3 oz) butter
225 g (8 oz) button mushrooms, thinly sliced
1 garlic clove, crushed
1 tsp dried oregano
salt and pepper
142 ml (5 fl oz) carton single cream

Bring the water to the boil in a large saucepan with the salt and oil. Add the tagliatelle and cook according to the packet instructions, until just tender, then drain well.

Meanwhile, melt the butter in a frying pan, add the mushrooms, garlic, oregano and salt and pepper and fry gently for 2-3 minutes.

Divide the pasta between 4 heated individual plates. Top each with the mushroom mixture and spoon over a portion of the cream immediately.

Serving idea: Serve with a large mixed salad dressing with vinaigrette.

● Fettuccine alla carbonara; Wholemeal spaghetti marinara; Tagliatelle with mushrooms and cream

---

Wholemeal spaghetti marinara

SERVES 4

1.5 litres (2½ pints) water
4 tbls vegetable oil
2 tsp salt
300 g (10 oz) wholemeal spaghetti
1 onion, chopped
300 ml (½ pint) dry white wine
1 garlic clove, crushed
284 ml (10 fl oz) carton double cream
2 tbls chopped chives
175 g (6 oz) peeled prawns, thawed if
  frozen
175 g (6 oz) canned mussels, drained
salt and pepper
grated Parmesan or any other hard
  cheese, to serve

Bring the water to the boil with 1 tbls of the oil and the salt in a large saucepan. Add the spaghetti and cook according to the packet instructions, until just tender, then drain.

Meanwhile, heat 2 tbls of the oil in a large frying pan, add the onion and fry gently for 5 minutes until softened. Add the wine and garlic and simmer until reduced by one-third.

Add the cream, chives, prawns and mussels to the pan. Heat through gently and season to taste.

Toss the spaghetti with the remaining oil. Divide between 4 heated individual plates and spoon over the seafood sauce. Serve immediately, with the Parmesan cheese handed separately in a bowl.

Fettuccine alla carbonara

SERVES 4

350 g (12 oz) fettuccine noodles
pinch of salt
3 tbls olive oil
1 onion, finely chopped
6 bacon rashers, rinded and chopped
6 tbls dry white wine
4 egg yolks
4 tbls double cream
75 g (3 oz) Parmesan cheese, grated
2 tbls chopped fresh parsley
1 garlic clove, crushed
salt and pepper

Cook the noodles in boiling, salted water for 8-10 minutes until just tender, then drain thoroughly.

Meanwhile, heat the oil in a frying pan, add the onion and fry gently for 5 minutes until softened. Add the bacon and fry for a further 2 minutes over high heat. Add the wine and allow the sauce to reduce.

In a small bowl, beat together the egg yolks, cream, Parmesan, parsley, garlic and salt and pepper.

Stir the bacon and cream mixtures into the hot noodles.

Serve immediately on heated plates.

Mackerel with gooseberry sauce

SERVES 4

4 mackerel, each about 350 g (12 oz),
   cleaned
salt and pepper
2 tbls lemon juice
lemon wedges, to garnish
For the sauce
225 g (8 oz) ripe gooseberries, topped
   and tailed
3 tbls boiling water
salt and pepper
pinch of ground ginger
1 tbls barbados sugar

To make the sauce, place all the sauce ingredients in a pan and cook gently, stirring, for about 5 minutes or until the gooseberries have become a pulp.

Cool slightly, then press through a fine nylon sieve. Return the sauce to the pan, reheat and adjust the seasoning to taste. Cover and set aside.

Pat the mackerel dry with absorbent paper. Make 3-4 diagonal slashes across the backbone on both sides of each mackerel, then season inside and out with salt and pepper and the lemon juice. Heat the grill to moderate.

Grill the mackerel for about 6 minutes on each side until cooked through and the flesh flakes easily when pierced with a sharp knife.

Arrange the mackerel on a heated serving dish and garnish with the lemon wedges. Hand the gooseberry sauce separately in a heated jug.

Serving ideas: Serve with new potatoes boiled in their skins.

Trout with mustard sauce

SERVES 4

4 rainbow trout, each about 350 g
    (12 oz), cleaned
salt and pepper
2 tbls vegetable oil
50 g (2 oz) butter
4 tbls chopped onion
142 ml (5 fl oz) carton single cream
2-4 tsp Dijon mustard
1 tsp lemon juice
To garnish
8 lemon slices
2 tbls chopped fresh parsley

Heat the grill to moderate.

Pat the trout dry with absorbent paper and season them inside.

Brush the trout with half the oil and grill for about 5 minutes on each side until they are cooked right through and the flesh flakes easily when pierced with a sharp knife.

Meanwhile, heat the butter with the remaining oil in a frying pan, add the onion and fry gently for 5 minutes until softened. Stir in the cream, mustard to taste, lemon juice and seasoning. Cook gently for 2-3 minutes without allowing to boil.

Arrange the trout on a heated serving dish and spoon over the mustard sauce. Arrange the lemon slices decoratively on the fish and sprinkle with the chopped parsley.

Serving ideas: Serve with boiled rice or mashed potatoes and steamed courgettes with herb butter.

● Left: Mackerel and gooseberry sauce; Right: Trout with mustard sauce

---

Scallop kebabs

SERVES 4

For the marinade
12 scallops, cleaned, thawed if
frozen, cut in half if large
175 g (6 oz) long-grain rice
175 g (6 oz) frozen peas
8 streaky bacon rashers, rinded,
halved lengthways and rolled up
50 g (2 oz) margarine or butter
100 g (4 oz) mushrooms, sliced
6 tbls vegetable oil
2 tbls white wine vinegar
2 tbls lemon juice
1 tsp paprika
1 tsp dried basil
salt and pepper

To make the marinade, combine the oil, vinegar, lemon juice, paprika, basil and salt and plenty of freshly ground black pepper in a shallow bowl.

Add the scallops to the marinade, turn to coat thoroughly and set aside while you cook the rice and peas.

Put the rice in a large saucepan of boiling salted water and cook for 12-15 minutes or until it is just tender. Then pour into a colander to drain.

Cook the peas in a separate saucepan of simmering salted water for about 5 minutes or until it is just tender, drain thoroughly.

Heat the grill to moderate.

Drain the scallops, reserving the marinade, and thread on to long kebab skewers alternately with the bacon rolls.

Cook under the grill for 8-10 minutes, turning the skewers several times and brushing the scallops and bacon with the remaining marinade, until the scallops are tender and cooked through and the bacon crisp.

Meanwhile, melt the margarine in a saucepan, add the mushrooms and fry gently for about 3 minutes, until soft.

Stir the rice and peas into the pan and season to taste.

Pile the rice mixture on to a heated serving dish and arrange the kebabs on top. Serve immediately.

• Scampi provençale; Scallop kebabs

Serving ideas: Serve with steamed green vegetables: courgettes, broccoli or tender green beans, lightly buttered and seasoned, or with Courgette bake (see page 35). A dry white wine such as Muscadet goes well with this dish.

Variations: Cubed cod or monk fish can be used instead of the scallops as can large, uncooked Dublin Bay prawns. Cherry tomatoes, pieces of onion or sweet pepper and button mushrooms all make tasty and attractive additions to the skewers.

Scampi provençale

SERVES 4

1 tbls vegetable oil
1 small onion, finely chopped
1 garlic clove, crushed
3 tomatoes, skinned and chopped
450 g (1 lb) scampi, thawed if frozen
   and well drained
2 tbls chopped fresh parsley
2 tbls dry white wine
salt and pepper
To garnish
8 lemon wedges
parsley sprigs

Heat the oil in a frying pan and add the onion and garlic. Fry gently for about 5 minutes until the onion is soft and lightly coloured.

Add the tomatoes, scampi, parsley and wine. Cook over moderate heat for 5-6 minutes until the scampi is cooked through. Season with a little salt and plenty of freshly ground black pepper.

Transfer to a heated serving dish, garnish with lemon wedges and parsley sprigs and serve immediately.

Serving ideas: Serve with boiled rice or sautéed potatoes and a mixed salad, accompanied by a chilled white wine.
Variation: To make a Prawn provençale substitute 450 g (1 lb) peeled prawns for the scampi.

31

Haddock flamenco

SERVES 4

750g (1½lb) haddock fillet, skinned
salt and pepper
25g (1 oz) butter
4 courgettes, sliced
1 onion, sliced
2 tomatoes, skinned and chopped
¼ tsp Tabasco sauce

Heat the oven to 200°C, 400°F, Gas Mark 6.

Cut the haddock into 4 equal pieces and season well.

Melt the butter in a frying pan, add the courgettes and onion and fry gently for 5 minutes until softened.

Add the tomatoes and Tabasco sauce and cook for a further 3 minutes, stirring occasionally.

Place the haddock pieces in a casserole, cover with the vegetable mixture and bake for 15-20 minutes or until the fish is cooked through and flakes easily when pierced with a sharp knife. Serve immediately.

Regal sole fillets

SERVES 4

340g (12 oz) can asparagus spears, drained
50g (2 oz) butter
1 shallot, finely chopped
4 lemon sole fillets, skinned
5 tbls dry white wine
5 tbls fish stock
142 ml (5 fl oz) carton double cream, lightly whipped
salt and pepper

Reserve 8 asparagus spears to garnish and finely chop the remainder.

Heat the oven to 180°C, 350°F, Gas Mark 4.

Grease an ovenproof dish with half the butter and sprinkle over the shallot. Set aside.

Lay the sole fillets flat, skinned side up. Divide the chopped asparagus among the fillets and roll them up.

Lay the rolled fillets seam side down on top of the shallot, pour over the wine and stock and cover with foil. Cook in the oven for about 15 minutes or until the fish flakes easily when tested with a small sharp knife.

Heat the grill to high. Transfer the fillets to a heated flameproof serving dish and keep warm. Pour the cooking liquid into a saucepan and boil until reduced by half, then remove the pan from the heat.

Add the remaining butter and stir until melted. Fold in the lightly whipped cream. Add some salt and plenty of freshly ground black pepper.

Pour the sauce over the fish and set under the grill for 2 minutes. Garnish with the reserved asparagus spears and serve immediately.

Serving idea: Serve with creamed potatoes and lightly steamed French beans well seasoned and buttered.

Fish pie with grapes

SERVES 4

450 g (1 lb) cod fillet
300 ml (½ pint) milk
300 ml (½ pint) water
1 bay leaf
salt and pepper
175 g (6 oz) green grapes, halved and
    seeded
142 ml (5 fl oz) carton double cream
450 g (1 lb) cooked, mashed potatoes
1 egg, beaten
2 tbls milk
100 g (4 oz) Cheddar or any other hard
    cheese, grated
25 g (1 oz) butter

Heat the oven to 180°C, 350°F, Gas Mark 4.

Place the cod in a saucepan and cover with the milk and water. Add the bay leaf and season to taste. Bring to the boil then reduce the heat, cover and simmer for about 8 minutes or until the fish is cooked and flakes easily when pierced with a sharp knife. Using a fish slice, transfer the cod to a plate and set aside.

Lightly grease a casserole and arrange the grapes over the base.

Flake cod and mix with the cream, salt and pepper. Place in the casserole.

Mix the potatoes with the egg and milk. Season well with salt and freshly ground pepper, spread over the fish, and fork a pattern on the potato. Or pipe the potato decoratively over the fish. Cover and bake for 20 minutes.

Heat the grill to moderate. Sprinkle the fish pie with the cheese, dot with the butter and place under the grill to brown.

• Left: Haddock flamenco; Centre: Fish pie with grapes; Right: Regal sole fillets

● Courgette bake; Speedy vegetable soufflé; Bean, bacon and tomato casserole

Speedy vegetable soufflé

SERVES 4

225 g (8 oz) cooked potatoes
100 g (4 oz) cooked cauliflower
100 g (4 oz) cooked carrots
4 tbls single cream
3 eggs, separated
100 g (4 oz) Cheddar or any other hard cheese, grated
salt and pepper

Heat the oven to 220°C, 425°F, Gas 7. Lightly grease an 18 cm (7 inch) soufflé dish or round deep ovenproof dish with butter or margarine.

In a bowl, finely mash together the potatoes, cauliflower and carrots and beat in the cream, egg yolks and cheese. Season to taste.

Whisk the egg whites stiffly. Using a large metal spoon, lightly, but thoroughly, fold them into the vegetable and cream mixture.

Spoon into the prepared dish and bake for 20 minutes, or until well risen and lightly coloured on top. Take out of the oven and serve immediately.

Serving idea: Serve as part of a vegetarian meal beginning with a tomato soup and following the soufflé with a mixed sweet pepper salad.
Variation: Use Brussels sprouts instead of cauliflower and swede instead of carrots.

34

gently for 5 minutes until softened, then add the garlic and fry for a further 2-3 minutes until the onion begins to brown.

Rinse and drain the courgettes, then pat dry with absorbent paper. Add to the frying pan and fry, turning from time to time, until lightly browned. Stir in the sausage and season to taste.

Place the mixture in a 1 litre (1¾ pint) ovenproof dish. Mix the cheeses and sprinkle over the top. Bake for about 25 minutes, until golden brown.

Serving idea: Serve with crusty wholemeal bread.
Variation: For a first course, bake in individual ovenproof dishes and reduce the cooking time by about 10 minutes.

Bean, bacon and tomato casserole

SERVES 4

2 tbls olive oil
4 streaky bacon rashers, rinded and diced
1 small onion, chopped
4 tbls chopped fresh parsley
2 tsp chopped fresh basil or 1 tsp dried basil
2 garlic cloves, crushed
2 × 198 g (7 oz) cans tomatoes
salt and pepper
198 g (7 oz) can white haricot beans, drained

Heat the oil in a flameproof casserole. Add the bacon, onion, parsley, basil and garlic and fry gently for 7 minutes until the onion is soft and golden.

Add the tomatoes with their juice and season with salt and pepper. Cover and simmer gently for 15 minutes.

Stir in the beans, cover and cook for a further 10 minutes. Serve hot.

Serving ideas: Serve the casserole with nutty brown rice as a light meal, or as an accompaniment to grilled or fried pork sausages.

Courgette bake

SERVES 4

450 g (1 lb) courgettes, sliced
salt
1 tbls vegetable oil
25 g (1 oz) margarine or butter
1 onion, chopped
1 garlic clove, crushed
100 g (4 oz) garlic sausage, sliced and chopped
pepper
50 g (2 oz) Cheddar cheese, grated
2 tbls grated Parmesan cheese

Heat the oven to 190°C, 375°F, Gas Mark 5.

Place the courgette slices in a colander, sprinkle with salt and set aside on a plate to drain for 20 minutes.

Heat the oil with the margarine in a large frying pan. Add the onion and fry

Cabbage and celery casserole

SERVES 4

75 g (3 oz) margarine
1 onion, sliced
1 head celery, sliced
½ head red or white cabbage,
  shredded
1 tbls wine vinegar
25 g (1 oz) plain flour
300 ml (½ pint) milk
salt and pepper
25 g (1 oz) fresh white breadcrumbs
25 g (1 oz) butter

Heat the oven to 180°C, 350°F, Gas Mark 4.

Melt 50 g (2 oz) of the margarine in a frying pan, add the onion and celery and cook gently for 5 minutes, stirring occasionally, until softened. Add the cabbage and vinegar and simmer for a further 5 minutes.

Meanwhile, melt the remaining margarine in a saucepan, add the flour and cook gently over low heat, stirring constantly, for 1 minute, without allowing the flour to colour. Remove from the heat and gradually stir in the milk. Return to the heat and cook, stirring, until the sauce is thickened and smooth. Season to taste.

Place the vegetable mixture in a 1 litre (2 pint) casserole and season with a little salt and plenty of pepper. Pour over the sauce, sprinkle with the breadcrumbs and dot with the butter.

Bake, uncovered, in the oven for 20 minutes until the topping is golden brown.

Serving ideas: Serve on its own with warmed herb bread or as an accompaniment to roast pork.
Variations: Two sliced carrots, steamed until just tender, can be added to the other vegetables in the casserole.

Lamb chops with mint butter

SERVES 4

4 loin or chump lamb chops, trimmed
fresh mint sprigs, to garnish
For the marinade
3 tbls vegetable oil
2 tbls dry cider or white wine
½ garlic clove, crushed
pepper
For the mint butter
50-75 g (2-3 oz) butter, softened
½ tsp wine vinegar
1 tbls chopped fresh mint
salt and pepper

Combine all the marinade ingredients in a shallow dish. Add the chops, turn to coat and leave to marinate at room temperature for 30 minutes, turning occasionally.

Heat the grill to high.

Remove the chops from the marinade and place on the grill rack. Grill for about 7 minutes on each side until the chops are done to your liking. Increase or lessen the grilling time according to the thickness of the chops.

Meanwhile, make the mint butter. Cream the butter in a bowl, then gradually work in the vinegar. Beat in the mint and salt and pepper, then shape into a roll on a piece of greaseproof paper. Chill until ready to serve, then cut into 4 slices.

When the chops are cooked, arrange on a heated serving dish, top each one with a pat of mint butter and garnish with mint sprigs.

Serving ideas: Serve with new potatoes boiled in their skins and broccoli or glazed carrots. Try adding a handful of raisins and 1 tsp of fennel seeds to the carrots for an unusual and delicious flavour.

● **Cabbage and celery casserole; Lamb chops with mint butter**

Lamb and fruit casserole

SERVES 4

8 small lamb loin chops
15 g (½ oz) margarine or butter
1 garlic clove, crushed
1 onion, chopped
1 tbls clear honey
½ tsp English mustard powder
1 small apple, diced
1 small piece fresh root ginger, chopped
50 g (2 oz) seedless raisins
150 ml (¼ pint) chicken stock
1 tsp cornflour
salt and pepper
To garnish
1 red apple, sliced
1 tbls lemon juice

Heat the oven to 160°C, 325°F, Gas Mark 3.

Heat the grill to high. Grill the chops for 2 minutes on each side, to brown.

Heat the margarine in a flameproof casserole, add the garlic and onion and fry gently for 5 minutes until softened. Add the honey and mustard, stir well to mix and remove from the heat.

Add the chops to the casserole, turn to coat and add the diced apple, ginger and raisins.

In a small saucepan blend the stock smoothly with the cornflour, season, bring to the boil and pour over the casserole. Cover and cook in the oven for 30 minutes, or until the chops are tender.

To serve, transfer to a heated serving dish and garnish with the apple slices dipped in the lemon juice.

● Lamb and fruit casserole; Lamb kebabs with barbecue sauce

Lamb kebabs with barbecue sauce

SERVES 4

*450 g (1 lb) boneless lamb, trimmed
    and cut into 2.5 cm (1 inch) cubes*
8 small tomatoes
12 mushrooms, trimmed
For the barbecue sauce
5 tbls lemon juice
5 tbls light soy sauce
4 tsp Worcestershire sauce
1 garlic clove, crushed
50 g (2 oz) margarine or butter
To serve
4 carrots, scraped and grated
½ small cabbage, shredded
2 small apples, diced
1 tsp lemon juice

Thread the lamb, tomatoes and mushrooms alternately on to 4 long kebab skewers. Set aside.

Make the barbecue sauce by combining all the ingredients in a small saucepan and stirring over gentle heat until the margarine has melted. Heat the grill to moderate.

Lay the kebabs on the grill rack and baste with the barbecue sauce. Cook under the grill for about 15 minutes, turning once or twice and basting frequently with the barbecue sauce, or until the lamb is tender.

Meanwhile, arrange the carrots, cabbage and apples, dipped in lemon juice, on a serving platter. Arrange the kebabs on top, reheat the remaining barbecue sauce and hand separately in a small jug.

Serving ideas: Serve with warmed pitta bread. In the summer, cook the kebabs on a barbecue, basting frequently with the sauce. If you make the sauce in advance, marinate the kebabs in it for 2 hours before cooking.

39

Turkey breasts in cider

SERVES 4

2 tbls vegetable oil
2 small onions, sliced
2 tbls plain flour
salt and pepper
2 turkey breasts, each about 225 g
  (8 oz), cut into 2.5 cm (1 inch) pieces
400 ml (14 fl oz) dry cider
3 large red peppers, cored, seeded and
  sliced
2 tbls single cream

Heat the oil in a large frying pan. Add the onions and fry gently for 5 minutes until softened.

Season the flour and toss the turkey meat in it, reserving any excess flour.

Add the turkey to the pan and fry over moderate heat for 4-5 minutes, turning, until golden brown on all sides. Remove the turkey pieces from the pan and set aside on a plate.

Add any reserved seasoned flour to the pan and cook for 1 minute, stirring constantly. Gradually pour in the cider, season and bring to the boil, stirring.

Return the turkey to the pan with the red peppers. Reduce the heat and simmer for 15-20 minutes, or until the turkey is cooked through.

Remove from the heat, stir in the cream, transfer to a heated serving dish and serve immediately.

Serving ideas: Serve with noodles and green salad. Spinach tagliatelle would add colour to the dish.

Creamed veal

SERVES 4

25 g (1 oz) butter
2 tbls vegetable oil
450-750 g (1-1½ lb) lean veal fillet,
thinly sliced
2 onions, finely chopped
225 g (8 oz) mushrooms, sliced
salt and pepper
142 ml (5 fl oz) carton double cream
4 tbls chopped fresh parsley
4 tsp chopped fresh mint
mint sprigs, to garnish

Heat the butter and oil in a large frying pan, add the veal and fry quickly to seal and brown on all sides. Remove the veal from the pan and set aside.

Add the onion to the pan and fry gently for about 10 minutes until soft and golden. Add the mushrooms and cook for a further 2-3 minutes.

Return the veal to the pan, season and cook gently for a further 2-3 minutes, or until the veal is tender and cooked through.

Stir in the cream, parsley and mint, and reheat gently. Transfer to a heated serving dish, garnish with the mint sprigs and serve immediately.

Serving ideas: Serve with sauté potatoes and chopped spinach, or on a bed of herb rice.

• Turkey breasts in cider; Creamed veal; Cheesy-topped burgers

Cheesy-topped burgers

SERVES 4-6

¾ kg (1½ lb) lean minced beef
50 g (2 oz) fresh white breadcrumbs
1 tsp dried mixed herbs
salt and pepper
1 egg, beaten
For the topping
90 g (3½ oz) full fat soft cheese
2 tbls chopped fresh chives
salt and pepper

Place the beef, breadcrumbs and herbs in a large mixing bowl and stir well to mix. Season and stir in the egg to bind.

Heat the grill to high.

Divide the beef mixture into 4-6 portions and shape each into a thick burger. Cook under the grill for about 8 minutes on each side until well-browned and cooked through. (If the burgers brown too quickly, reduce the grill to moderate.)

Meanwhile, beat the topping ingredients in a bowl until soft and well blended.

Remove the burgers from the grill. Spoon a portion of the topping mixture on to each one and return to the grill to heat through. Serve immediately.

Stuffed peppers

SERVES 4

4 medium peppers (green, yellow or
    red)
salt and pepper
275 g (10 oz) lean minced beef
1 medium onion, chopped
50 g (2 oz) mushrooms, sliced
3 tomatoes, chopped
1 slice bread, toasted and cubed
1/4 tsp Worcestershire sauce

Heat the oven to 180°C, 350°F, Gas
Mark 4.

Cut off and reserve the tops of the
peppers and remove the core and seeds.
Cook the peppers for 5 minutes in a
large saucepan of boiling salted water.
Drain and season well inside.

Place the beef with the onion in a
non-stick frying pan and fry without
added fat, stirring, until the meat is
evenly browned. Stir in the
mushrooms, tomatoes, bread cubes
and Worcestershire sauce and season
to taste.

Spoon the mixture into the peppers
and replace the tops. Place upright in a
baking dish and bake in the oven about
25 minutes until tender.

Serving ideas: Serve the stuffed peppers hot on a bed of rice, or cold with a
selection of salads, for lunch or supper.
Variations: The minced beef may be
replaced with minced pork or with
finely chopped chicken.

Gammon steaks with parsley sauce

SERVES 4

4 smoked gammon steaks, each
    about 175 g (6 oz), rinded
25 g (1 oz) melted margarine or butter
For the sauce
142 ml (5 fl oz) carton soured cream
4 tbls chopped fresh parsley
1 tsp French mustard
salt and pepper
parsley sprigs, to garnish

Heat the grill to moderate.

Snip the fat at 1 cm (1/2 inch) intervals
around the gammon steaks.

Brush the steaks on one side with
margarine and cook under the grill for 5
minutes. Turn the steaks, brush with
more margarine and cook for a further
3-5 minutes, or until cooked through.
Transfer to a heated serving dish and
keep warm in a low oven.

To make the sauce, place all the ingredients in a small saucepan and stir
over gentle heat until heated through,
but on no account allow to boil.

Pour the sauce over the gammon
steaks, garnish with parsley sprigs and
serve immediately.

Serving ideas: Serve with new potatoes and French beans. Grilled
mushrooms also go well with this dish:
use large open mushrooms and brush
them liberally with melted butter.

• Stuffed peppers; Gammon steaks with parsley sauce; Spicy shepherd's pie

Spicy shepherd's pie

SERVES 4

15 g (½oz) margarine or butter
1 onion, chopped
25 g (1 oz) plain flour
300 ml (½ pint) hot beef stock
450 g (1 lb) cooked lamb, minced
1 tbls Worcestershire sauce
pinch of grated nutmeg
good pinch of mild curry powder
salt and pepper
220 g (7¾ oz) can baked beans in
   tomato sauce
1 lb cooked potatoes, mashed
parsley sprigs, to garnish

Melt the margarine in a saucepan, add the onion and fry gently for 5 minutes, until softened. Stir in the flour and cook for 1 minute, stirring.

Remove the pan from the heat and stir in the stock and minced lamb. Add the Worcestershire sauce, nutmeg and curry powder and season to taste.

Return to the heat and bring to the boil, then simmer for 20 minutes. Add the baked beans and cook for a further 5 minutes. Heat the grill to moderate.

Transfer to a heated flameproof dish. Spread the mashed potatoes evenly over the spicy lamb mixture and fork a pattern on the surface. Place under the grill until golden brown. Garnish with parsley sprigs and serve immediately.

Serving ideas: Serve with buttered sprouts or glazed carrots.

43

Piquant spare rib chops

SERVES 4

4 pork spare rib chops
1 tbls vegetable oil
salt and pepper
For the sauce
2 tbls vegetable oil
1 onion, finely chopped
198 g (7 oz) can peeled tomatoes
4 tbls soft light brown sugar
4 tbls red wine vinegar
2 tbls tomato ketchup
2 tsp light soy sauce

To make the sauce, heat the oil in a small saucepan, add the onion and fry gently for 5 minutes, until softened.

Add the tomatoes with their juice, breaking them up with a wooden spoon, and the remaining sauce ingredients. Bring to the boil, then lower the heat and simmer, uncovered, for about 10 minutes until reduced.

Meanwhile, pat the pork chops dry with absorbent paper, rub both sides with oil and season.

Heat the grill to high. Arrange the chops in a flameproof serving dish and brown for 1 minute on each side under the grill.

Pour the sauce over the chops, reduce the heat and grill as far away from the heat as possible for about 8-10 minutes on each side, basting several times with the sauce. Serve the pork chops straight from the dish.

Serving ideas: Serve with boiled rice or jacket potatoes and a green salad. Or be different and serve baked sweet potatoes, an orange, watercress and lettuce salad and steamed baby sweetcorn, tossed in a little butter and well seasoned with salt and pepper.

Risotto with leeks and bacon

SERVES 4

450 g (1 lb) streaky bacon rashers,
  rinded and chopped
4 tbls vegetable oil
4 leeks, trimmed and chopped
450 g (1 lb) long-grain rice
397 g (14 oz) can tomatoes
1 tsp salt
1 tsp pepper
½ tsp cayenne pepper
½ tsp ground cumin
1 tsp grated lemon rind
900 ml (1½ pints) strong,
  well-flavoured chicken stock
15 g (½ oz) butter
grated Parmesan cheese, to serve

Fry the bacon in a large non-stick saucepan without added fat for 6-8 minutes or until crisp and brown. Remove with a slotted spoon, drain on absorbent paper and set aside.

Heat the oil in the pan. Add the leeks and fry gently for 10 minutes, stirring from time to time. Add the rice and fry for a further 5 minutes, stirring often.

Add the tomatoes with their juice, salt and pepper, cayenne, cumin, lemon rind and stock and bring to the boil, stirring.

Return the bacon to the pan and simmer for 15-20 minutes, or until the rice is cooked and all the liquid has been absorbed.

Pile on to a heated serving dish, fork in the butter and serve with the Parmesan cheese handed separately.

• Piquant spare rib chops; Risotto with leeks and bacon

● Top left: Cinzano kidneys; Bottom: Peppery steak; Right: Spanish pork chops

Cinzano kidneys

SERVES 4

225 g (8 oz) mushrooms, sliced
2 tsp lemon juice
25 g (1 oz) margarine or butter
8 lamb's kidneys, cored, skinned and
　quartered
salt and pepper
1 tbls flour
150 ml (¼ pint) white Cinzano
2 tbls single cream
2 tbls chopped fresh parsley, to
　garnish

Heat the oven to 160°C, 325°F, Gas
Mark 3. Sprinkle the mushrooms with
the lemon juice.

Melt the margarine in a frying pan,
add the kidneys and fry quickly, stirring, to brown on all sides. Add the
mushrooms and cook for a further 3
minutes. Season to taste. Sprinkle over
the flour and cook for 1 minute.

Place the kidneys and mushrooms in
a casserole, pour over the Cinzano,
cover and bake 20 minutes.

Adjust the seasoning to taste. Swirl
the cream over the top, garnish with
the chopped parsley and serve straight
from the casserole.

Serving ideas: Serve on a bed of hot
boiled rice or with creamed potatoes
accompanied by a green salad.

spoon and place in a casserole.

Heat the oil in the frying pan, add the onion and fry gently for 5 minutes until softened. Remove from the pan with a slotted spoon and add to the casserole.

Dust the pork chops with the seasoned flour. Add to the frying pan and fry quickly on both sides to brown and seal, then add to the casserole. Combine the wine and tomato purée and pour over the chops.

Cover the casserole and cook in the oven for 25 minutes, then stir in the olives, reserving a few to garnish.

Garnish the chops with hard-boiled egg slices topped with olive slices and serve straight from the casserole.

Peppery steak

SERVES 4

4 sirloin steaks, about 100 g (4 oz)
each, trimmed
black peppercorns, crushed, to taste
1 tablespoon melted butter
For the sauce
284 ml (10 fl oz) carton double cream
2 tbls brandy
salt and pepper
watercress sprigs, to garnish

Heat the grill to high. Sprinkle the steaks on one side with half the crushed peppercorns. Using a meat mallet or rolling pin, pound the steaks so that the peppercorns adhere. Turn the steaks and coat them in the same way on the other side with the remaining peppercorns.

Brush the steaks with butter and cook under the grill until cooked to your liking, turning several times and brushing with more butter.

Transfer the steaks to a heated serving dish.

To make the sauce, place the cream in a small saucepan and add the brandy and salt and freshly ground black pepper. Heat gently, stirring, until bubbles start to appear, then pour over the steaks. Garnish with watercress sprigs and serve immediately.

Spanish pork chops

SERVES 4

4 rashers smoked bacon, rinded and
chopped
1 tbls vegetable oil
1 onion, chopped
4 pork chops, trimmed, with kidneys
1 tbls plain flour, seasoned with
salt and pepper
150 ml (¼ pint) red wine
1 tbls tomato purée
20 stuffed olives, sliced
2 hard-boiled eggs, sliced, to garnish

Heat the oven to 190°C, 375°F, Gas Mark 5.

Fry the bacon in a large non-stick frying pan without added fat for about 5 minutes, then remove with a slotted

47

Liver with orange

SERVES 4

1 tbls vegetable oil
15g (¹/₂oz) margarine or butter
1 onion, chopped
1 garlic clove, crushed
2 tablespoons plain flour
salt and pepper
450g (1 lb) lambs' liver, sliced
450 ml (³/₄ pint) well-flavoured
   chicken stock
2 tsp soft dark brown sugar
2 oranges, peeled and thinly sliced
2 tbls chopped chives, to garnish

Heat the oil and margarine in a large frying pan. Add the onion and garlic and cook gently for 5 minutes until softened.

Season the flour and use to dust the liver. Add the liver to the frying pan and fry quickly, turning, to brown on all sides. Gradually stir in the stock with the sugar and bring just to the boil.

Lower the heat and simmer gently for about 10 minutes or until the liver is tender but still slightly pink inside.

Add the orange slices to the pan and adjust the seasoning to taste. Arrange the liver and oranges on a heated serving dish, spoon over the sauce and garnish with the chives.

● Left: Chicken pilaff
Centre: Liver with orange
Right: Chicken with walnuts

Chicken pilaff

SERVES 4

25g (1 oz) margarine or butter
4 bacon rashers, rinded and diced
1 onion, chopped
225g (8 oz) long-grain rice
600 ml (1 pint) chicken stock
salt and pepper
1 bay leaf
50g (2 oz) sultanas
25g (1 oz) toasted almonds, chopped
350g (12 oz) cooked chicken meat,
   boned and skinned, and cut into
   bite-sized pieces
grated Parmesan or any other hard
   cheese, to serve

Melt the margarine in a large saucepan, add the bacon and onion and fry gently for 5 minutes until softened.

Stir in the rice, stock and salt and pepper. Add the bay leaf and bring to the boil. Cover and simmer gently for 20 minutes until the rice is tender and all the liquid has been absorbed.

Add the sultanas, almonds and chicken and cook gently, uncovered, for a further 5 minutes.

Pile onto a heated serving dish and serve immediately, with grated Parmesan cheese handed separately.

Serving ideas: Serve with a vegetable curry or mixed salad.

Chicken with walnuts

SERVES 4

50 g (2 oz) butter
4 chicken breasts, boned and skinned
1 leek, trimmed and sliced
4 button onions, peeled
450 ml (¾ pint) chicken stock
1 sprig fresh thyme or ½ tsp dried
    thyme
2 tbls white wine vinegar
salt and pepper
75 g (3 oz) walnuts, finely chopped
1 tbls single cream
2 tbls chopped fresh parsley, to
    garnish

Melt the butter in a large frying pan,
add the chicken breasts and fry, turning until golden brown on all sides.
Remove the chicken with a slotted
spoon and set aside.

Add the leek and onions to the pan
and cook gently for 5 minutes until
softened.

Return the chicken to the pan with
all the remaining ingredients. Cover
and cook over moderate heat for 15
minutes or until the chicken is cooked
through.

Transfer the chicken to a heated
serving dish and keep warm.

Place the vegetables and walnuts
from the pan in a blender with a little of
the cooking liquid. Process until
smooth. (Vary the amount of cooking
liquid used according to the desired
consistency of the sauce.)

Return the sauce to the frying pan,
adjust the seasoning to taste and stir
over moderate heat until heated
through, without boiling.

Pour the sauce over the chicken
breasts and garnish with the chopped
parsley. Serve immediately.

49

Chicken and apple salad

SERVES 4

*283 g (10 oz) can potatoes, drained
  and sliced*
2 tbls mayonnaise
350 g (12 oz) cooked chicken, diced
2 red dessert apples, cored and sliced
100 g (4 oz) cooked ham, diced
1 tsp dried mixed herbs
2 tbls lemon juice
salt and pepper
1 small cos lettuce or curly endive
a little paprika, to finish

Place the potatoes in a large mixing bowl. Add the mayonnaise and toss gently to coat.

Add the chicken, apple slices, ham, herbs, lemon juice and salt and freshly ground black pepper to the potatoes and toss gently but thoroughly.

Cover with cling film and refrigerate for 25-30 minutes.

To serve, line a shallow serving dish with lettuce leaves or endive, pile the chicken salad in the centre and sprinkle with paprika.

Serving ideas: Serve as part of a selection of salads for a summer buffet or as a light lunch by itself, with a glass of chilled white wine.

Variations: Make a Chicken and celery salad by substituting 4 thinly sliced celery stalks for the apples. A handful of raisins is a good addition for either version.

● Left: Greek salad; Centre: Chicken and apple salad; Right Salami pasta salad

Greek salad

SERVES 4

1 cos lettuce
1 bunch of radishes, trimmed and
    sliced
½ large cucumber, diced
225 g (8 oz) feta cheese, cubed
good pinch of dried marjoram
4 tomatoes, skinned and sliced
6 canned anchovy fillets, drained
    and finely chopped
12 large black olives
1 tbls chopped fresh parsley
pepper
For the dressing
4 tbls olive oil
4 tsp white wine vinegar
1 tbls chopped fresh herbs
4 spring onions, finely chopped
1 tsp sugar
salt and pepper

Separate the lettuce into leaves and
thoroughly wash under cold running
water. Dry thoroughly, then tear into
pieces and arrange on a large serving
platter. Scatter the radish slices and
diced cucumber over the top.

Arrange the cheese in the centre and
sprinkle with the marjoram. Arrange
the tomato slices around the cheese
and top with the anchovies and olives.
Sprinkle with the parsley and season
with pepper.

Cover with cling film and chill in the
refrigerator until ready to serve.

To make the dressing, combine all
the ingredients in a screw-top jar and
shake vigorously until thoroughly
blended.

When ready to serve, pour the
dressing over the salad.

Salami pasta salad

SERVES 4

100 g (4 oz) pasta bows or twists
1 tbls vegetable oil
100 g (4 oz) salami, rinded and
    chopped
198 g (7 oz) can sweetcorn, drained
3 celery stalks, chopped
12 green or black olives
1 small red pepper, cored, seeded and
    chopped
1 tbls chopped fresh parsley
1 tbls chopped fresh basil
For the dressing
3 tbls vegetable oil
1 tbls lemon juice
salt and pepper

Cook the pasta in boiling, salted water
with the oil for 10 minutes or until just
tender. Drain and rinse under cold running water, then drain again.

Allow the pasta to cool, then combine
with the remaining salad ingredients
in a large salad bowl.

Place the ingredients for the dressing
in a screw-top jar, and shake vigorously
until thoroughly blended.

Pour the dressing over the salad and
toss well to coat all the ingredients.
Cover with cling film and chill in the
refrigerator until ready to serve. Toss
again just before serving.

● Seafood rice salad

Seafood rice salad

SERVES 4

350 g (12 oz) cold cooked rice
1 celery stalk, thinly sliced
225 g (8 oz) peeled prawns
50 g (2 oz) thick mayonnaise
1 tsp grated lemon rind
salt and pepper
pinch of paprika
8 lettuce leaves, washed

Place the rice, celery and prawns, reserving a few for the garnish, in a large mixing bowl.

Add the mayonnaise and lemon rind and toss gently until all the ingredients are coated. Season with salt, pepper and paprika.

Line a salad bowl with the lettuce leaves, pile the salad into the centre and garnish with the reserved prawns.

Serving idea: For a summer picnic, serve with buttered wholemeal bread.
Variations: Fresh crab meat may be substituted for the prawns and the salad can be 'stretched' by adding 100 g (4 oz) cooked peas. For more piquancy add 3 oz (75 g) sliced stuffed olives.

DESSERTS

Cherries jubilee

SERVES 4

2 × 425g (15oz) cans stoned black
   cherries, drained and syrup
   reserved
4 tbls redcurrant jelly
4 tbls orange juice
grated rind of 1 orange
3 tbls brandy
142 ml (5 fl oz) carton double cream,
   whipped
4 orange slices, to decorate

Place the cherries in a bowl. Combine 6 tbls of the reserved cherry syrup with the redcurrant jelly and orange juice and rind in a small saucepan. Stir over low heat to dissolve the jelly.

Add the brandy and cherries to the pan and quickly bring to the boil.

Carefully set light to the surface with a match and gently shake the pan until the flames subside.

Spoon the cherries into individual glass serving bowls and pour over the syrup to cover. Decorate with orange twists and serve with the whipped cream.

Barbados bananas

SERVES 4

4 firm bananas, peeled
1 tsp rum essence
150 ml (¼ pint) orange juice
1 tbls dark brown sugar
15 g (½ oz) butter, diced
toasted nuts, to garnish
whipped cream, for serving cold

Heat the oven to 180°C, 350°F, Gas Mark 4. Cut the bananas in half lengthways. Place in a shallow ovenproof dish and pour over the rum essence and orange juice. Sprinkle the brown sugar over the bananas and top with the butter.

Cover and bake for 20-30 minutes, or until the bananas are soft. Sprinkle with the toasted nuts. Serve hot, or cold with piped cream.

• Cherries jubilee; Barbados bananas

Zabaglione

SERVES 4-6

4 egg yolks
2 egg whites
4 tbls caster sugar
4 tbls Marsala

Place a 2.5 litre (4½ pint) heatproof mixing bowl over a large saucepan of water. Fill the saucepan with enough water to immerse the base of the bowl. Remove the bowl from the pan. Bring the water to the boil, then reduce the heat to simmering point.

Place all the ingredients in the bowl and set over the simmering water. Using an electric hand-held beater, set to highest speed and whisk for about 5 minutes until the mixture is very thick, frothy and leaves a trail when the beaters are lifted. (It is important not to let the water boil or the mixture will begin to cook on the sides of the bowl.)

Spoon into individual wine glasses and serve immediately.

Serving ideas: Serve with sweet wafer biscuits or shortbread fingers.
Variation: Marsala is the traditional Italian ingredient but sweet sherry may be used instead.

Pineapple boats

SERVES 4

2 small fresh pineapples
225 g (8 oz) seedless grapes, halved
300 ml (½ pint) double cream
25 g (1 oz) desiccated coconut
extra grapes, to decorate

Cut the pineapples in half lengthways; using a sharp knife, carefully remove the flesh and cut into chunks. Do the

54

Summer fool

SERVES 4

*225 g (8 oz) strawberries, washed and
hulled*
*225 g (8 oz) raspberries, washed and
hulled*
75-100 g (3-4 oz) icing sugar, sifted
*284 ml (10 fl oz) carton double cream,
lightly whipped*

Purée the strawberries and raspberries
in a blender and press through a fine
nylon sieve to remove all the seeds.

Sweeten the fruit purée to taste with
the icing sugar.

Using a large metal spoon, gently,
but thoroughly, fold the whipped
cream into the fruit purée.

Pour into 4 individual glass bowls
and chill in the refrigerator until ready
to serve.

Serving ideas: Very thinly slice some
extra strawberries and arrange on the
top of each serving. Serve with shortbread fingers.

● Left to right: Zabaglione; Summer fool;
Pineapple boats; Melon salad bowl

Melon salad bowl

SERVES 4

*2 ripe honeydew melons, halved and
seeded*
½ tsp ground ginger
To decorate
mint sprigs
½-1 tbls caster sugar

Remove as much of the melon flesh as
you can with a melon baller or teaspoon, using a dish to catch the juice.

Scoop out what is left of the melon
flesh and purée in a blender. Combine
with the melon balls and stir in the
ginger.

Cover with cling film and chill in the
refrigerator until ready to serve.

To serve, place the melon mixture in
individual bowls and sprinkle with the
caster sugar to taste. Garnish with the
mint sprigs.

cutting over a bowl to catch the juice.

Combine the halved grapes with the
pineapple in a bowl.

Whip the cream until it forms soft
peaks. Gently fold in the coconut, then
fold in the pineapple and grapes.

Spoon the fruit and cream mixture
into the pineapple shells and decorate
with grapes.

Chill in the refrigerator until ready to
serve.

Variations: 25 ml (2 fl oz) white rum
may be added to the grapes and pineapples before they are folded into the
cream. If fresh pineapples are not available, make the dessert with well-
drained canned pineapple chunks and
serve in individual glass bowls.

Chestnut creams

SERVES 4-6

425 g (15 oz) can sweetened chestnut purée
1 tbls finely grated orange rind plus a little extra, to decorate
284 ml (10 fl oz) carton double cream plus a little extra, to decorate
2 egg whites
2 tbls chopped blanched almonds

In a bowl, mix together the chestnut purée, orange rind and 4 tbls of cream.

Whisk the remaining cream until it forms soft peaks and fold into the chestnut mixture.

Whisk the egg whites until stiff, then fold into the mixture.

Spoon the chestnut cream into individual glasses, top with cream, and chill in the refrigerator.

When ready to serve sprinkle with the chopped nuts and top with a little orange rind

Serving ideas: Decorate with whipped cream and marrons glacés.

Baked strawberry Alaska

SERVES 4

½ jam Swiss roll, sliced
227 g (8 oz) can strawberries, drained and syrup reserved
small block vanilla ice cream
2 large egg whites
100 g (4 oz) caster sugar
To decorate
4 strips candied angelica
4 glacé cherries, halved

Heat the oven to 230°C, 450°F, Gas Mark 8.

Arrange the Swiss roll slices in a circle on a flat ovenproof plate, pressing the slices close together.

Spoon over a little of the strawberry syrup to moisten the cake. Place the vanilla ice cream in the centre over the cake and pile the strawberries on top.

Whisk the egg whites until stiff, then gradually whisk in half the sugar, until the meringue is stiff and glossy. Fold in the remaining sugar.

Quickly spread the meringue over the cake, fruit and ice cream so that they are completely covered.

Bake in the oven for 2-3 minutes until the meringue is lightly coloured. Remove from the oven, decorate with the candied angelica and glacé cherries and serve immediately.

Serving idea: For special occasions, serve this dessert with a chilled bottle of a white dessert wine, such as a Sauternes.

Banana pancakes with maple syrup

SERVES 4

100 g (4 oz) plain flour
½ tsp salt
2 eggs, beaten
300 ml (½ pint) milk
1 tsp vegetable oil
extra vegetable oil, for frying
150 ml (¼ pint) maple syrup
25 g (1 oz) butter, melted
sliced banana, to decorate
For the filling
4 ripe bananas
50 g (2 oz) icing sugar
finely grated rind of 2 oranges

To make the batter, sift the flour with the salt into a mixing bowl and make a well in the centre. Pour in the eggs and gradually pour in the milk, drawing in the flour with a wooden spoon, to make a smooth batter. Stir in 1 tsp oil.

Heat a little oil in a 15 cm (6 inch) frying pan until very hot, wiping off any excess with absorbent paper. Pour in enough batter to cover the base thinly, tilting the pan so it is evenly coated.

Cook until the pancake is golden brown on the underside, then turn over with a fish slice and cook until golden on the other side.

Transfer the pancake to a heated plate and keep warm. Fry the remaining batter in the same way, stacking the pancakes as they are cooked with a piece of greaseproof paper between each one.

To make the filling, peel and mash the bananas in a bowl with the icing sugar and orange rind.

Pour the maple syrup into a small saucepan and heat until very hot. Spoon a portion of the filling on to one half of each pancake, dividing it equally among them. Roll up the pancakes.

Brush a serving dish with the butter. Arrange the rolled pancakes in the dish. Decorate with the sliced banana, pour over the hot maple syrup and serve.

● Chestnut creams; Banana pancakes with maple syrup; Baked strawberry Alaska

● Left to right; Fruit and nut crumble; Bittersweet chocolate fruit sundaes; Hot fudge sundaes

Fruit and nut crumble

SERVES 4

750 g (1 1/2 lb) fresh cherries, stoned
and chopped
4 tbls barbados sugar
150 g (5 oz) plain wholemeal flour
1/2 tsp ground cardamom
1/2 tsp ground mixed spice
1 tsp ground cinnamon
1/2 tsp grated nutmeg
75 g (3 oz) margarine or butter, diced
50 g (2 oz) Brazil nuts, chopped

Heat the oven to 200°C, 400°F, Gas Mark 6.

Place the cherries in a bowl, sprinkle with 1 tbls of the sugar and set aside.

Mix the flour and spices together in a mixing bowl, add the margarine and rub in with the fingertips until the mixture resembles fine breadcrumbs. Stir in the remaining sugar.

Lightly grease an ovenproof serving dish. Spoon one-third of the crumble mixture into the base. Place half the cherries and any juice on top and sprinkle over half the remaining crumble mixture. Repeat the layers once more so that all the ingredients are used. Scatter the chopped Brazil nuts over the top of the crumble.

Cover with foil and bake in the oven for 15 minutes, then remove the foil and bake for a further 10 minutes. Serve straight from the dish.

Serving ideas: Serve with custard or whipped cream.

Bittersweet chocolate fruit sundaes

SERVES 4

142 ml (5 fl oz) carton double cream
2 tbls strong black coffee
100 g (4 oz) plain chocolate, broken into pieces
85 ml (3 fl oz) apricot jam
8 scoops tutti-frutti ice cream or your favourite flavour

Place the double cream, black coffee chocolate and jam in a small saucepan over very low heat. Stir until the chocolate and jam are melted and the sauce is smooth and blended. Do not allow the sauce to boil.

Strain the sauce through a sieve, pressing it through with a spoon.

Serve either warm or cold over scoops of ice cream.

Hot fudge sundaes

SERVES 4

50 g (2 oz) plain chocolate, broken into pieces
40 g (1½ oz) unsalted butter
1½ tbls liquid glucose
85 ml (3 fl oz) boiling water
25 ml (1 fl oz) strong black coffee
150 g (5 oz) soft dark brown sugar
50 g (2 oz) caster sugar
2-3 drops vanilla essence
pinch of salt
8 scoops vanilla ice cream

Place all the ingredients except the ice cream in a small saucepan and stir over a gentle heat until the chocolate is melted and the sauce is smooth.

Bring to the boil and cook, stirring, for 3 minutes.

Pour over the ice cream and serve.

Lemon snow

SERVES 6

300 ml (½ pint) cold water
15 g (½ oz) powdered gelatine
100 g (4 oz) caster sugar
thinly pared rind and juice of
    2 lemons
3 egg whites

candied peel, to decorate
150 ml (¼ pint) whipped cream, to
    serve

Pour the water into a saucepan and sprinkle the gelatine on top. Leave to soak for 5 minutes.

Stir in the sugar and the lemon rind. Place the pan over low heat and stir until both the gelatine and sugar have dissolved. Do not allow the mixture to boil.

Strain the mixture into a large bowl and set aside until cold.

Stand the bowl in a basin of cold water and ice cubes. Strain the lemon juice and add to the gelatine mixture along with the egg whites. Using a rotary beater or a hand held electric beater, beat the mixture until thick and white and on the point of setting – this may take up to 10 minutes.

Pour the mixture into a serving dish and leave in the refrigerator until set.

Decorate with the candied peel and serve with the whipped cream.

Variation: Other citrus fruits may be used instead of lemons – limes, for instance, or orange. If using orange, use 1 large fruit and reduce the amount of sugar by half.

Serving ideas: Serve with brandy snaps, almond tuiles or other light biscuits.

Chocolate mousse

SERVES 4-6

224 g (8 oz) plain chocolate, broken
into bits
4 tbls black coffee or rum
150 ml (¼ pint) whipping cream
4 eggs, separated
grated chocolate, to decorate

Put the chocolate and coffee or rum in a heatproof bowl placed over, but not in, a pan of barely simmering water and stir to melt.

When the chocolate has melted, remove the pan from the heat and beat in the egg yolks, one at a time, mixing one in thoroughly before adding the next. Set aside to cool.

Whip the cream until thick and fold it into the chocolate mixture.

Whip the egg whites until stiff and fold in quickly and thoroughly.

Pour the mixture into small pots, cover and refrigerate until the mousse is set.

Decorate with the grated chocolate before serving.

Serving ideas: Serve with light biscuits and after a light meal – this is a rich mixture.

Variation: Substitute brandy for the black coffee or rum. Add the juice and grated rind from ½ orange to the mixture with the egg yolks.

● Lemon snow; Chocolate mousse

Pears with port and orange sauce

SERVES 4

200 ml (⅓ pint) port
1 tbls grated orange rind
120 ml (4 fl oz) orange juice
120 ml (4 fl oz) water
6 tbls sugar
4 firm ripe pears

Place the port, orange rind and juice and water in a saucepan large enough to hold the four pears upright. Bring to the boil, add the sugar and stir until it is dissolved.

Carefully peel the pears, leaving the stalks intact.

Add the pears to the pan and turn to coat in the syrup. Stand the pears upright and simmer gently, basting frequently with syrup, for about 10 minutes or until tender but not mushy.

Arrange the pears on a serving dish. Boil the sauce rapidly until reduced by about half. Pour the sauce over the pears, cool, then chill in the refrigerator until ready to serve.

Serving idea: Serve with a bowl of slightly sweetened whipped cream.
Variation: Red wine may be substituted for the port. For special occasions, the pears may be sprinkled with toasted flaked almonds.

• Creamy fruit cups; Pears with port and orange sauce; Apple brûlée

Apple brûlée

SERVES 4

1 kg (2 lb) cooking apples, peeled, cored and sliced
4 tbls water
75-100 g (3-4 oz) sugar
284 ml (10 fl oz) carton double cream
2 tsp finely grated orange rind
about 6 tbls soft light brown sugar

Cook the apples with the water in a saucepan for 10-15 minutes, stirring occasionally, until soft, then cook for a further 5 minutes or until reduced to a thick purée. Sweeten to taste.

Pour into a flameproof serving dish and set aside to cool.

Whip the cream until thick and gently fold in the orange rind. Spoon evenly over the fruit and chill in the refrigerator until required.

When ready to serve, heat the grill to high. Cover the cream with a layer of brown sugar 1 cm (⅔ inch) thick.

Set under the grill until the sugar melts and caramelizes. Allow the topping to cool and harden, then serve.

Creamy fruit cups

SERVES 4

*312 g (11 oz) can mandarin oranges,
    drained, syrup reserved
312 g (11 oz) can apricot halves,
    drained, syrup reserved
142 ml (5 fl oz) carton double cream
1 tbls caster sugar
freshly grated nutmeg, to finish*

Reserve 8 mandarin segments for decoration and chop the remaining mandarins and apricots. Place the chopped fruit in the base of the 4 individual glass dessert bowls or in a large bowl.

In a bowl, combine the cream, sugar and 85 ml (3 fl oz) of the mixed fruit syrups. Beat until it forms soft peaks.

Spoon the cream mixture over the top of the fruit salads. Decorate each with 2 orange segments and sprinkle with nutmeg. Chill in the refrigerator for up to 1 hour before serving.

Serving idea: This very sweet dessert is best after a light main course, such as roast chicken.

Variations: Add finely grated orange rind to the cream mixture, for a tangier taste. This dessert may be made with any combination of canned fruit available. For a more sophisticated flavour use lychees, guavas and mangoes and replace the fruit syrup with brandy.

INDEX

Note: this index includes variations suggested in recipes as well as the main recipes.